Retaining Ruby: Start Learning Ruby Today, Even If You've Never Coded Before (A Beginner's Guide)

Disclaimer and Terms of Use: Effort has been made to ensure that the information in this book is accurate and complete, however, the author and the publisher do not warrant the accuracy of the information, text and graphics contained within the book due to the rapidly changing nature of science, research, known and unknown facts and internet. The Author and the publisher do not hold any responsibility for errors, omissions or contrary interpretation of the subject matter herein. This book is presented solely for motivational and informational purposes only.

Table of Contents

Introduction

Today's society is a fast-paced, instant gratification kind of world. Everyone wants results immediately and most have some form of technology in their homes. Computers are considered to be some of the twenty first century's most wondrous achievements. Computers are now in everything we do—they are literally everywhere from traffic light sensors to GPS locator chips that end up being implanted into animals in case that animal gets lost. Now, one can even obtain a watch that can be synchronized with one's cell phone in order to remain completely plugged into social media. But, how is this possible? What 'magic' and science allows this technology to happen? It is known that computers cannot function by themselves. A computer programmer is often responsible for typing in a sort of syntactical code to create a program. When that program is ran, the computer then translates that code into a language that the computer can understand thus allowing the computer to execute the function or functions desired by the program.

Computer programming seems a daunting task at first—that is, until one simply opens a book and begins to read. There is not a lot that an individual cannot do with programming if one is simply intelligent enough to read and follow directions. Computer programming on the whole is just a process. The person is introduced to a computer programming problem. The procedure for solving any problem is the same for computer programming. Those steps are: analysis, development of understanding, generating algorithms, verification that those algorithms are correct, and implementation. In computer speak, implementation is simply the act of coding. There are many different source codes in which an individual can utilize during the final step of implementation. The reason behind the existence of the concept of programming is simple. Programmers simply find a set of instructions that will allow the computer to automatically perform a specific task or to solve a problem, such as in mathematics. Though the process of programming often requires that a person be well-read and possess a superlative understanding in application domain, specialized algorithms, and formal logic, it does not always require seeking higher education. As previously stated, one can simply obtain a book and learn on one's own without an instructor—especially this day and age in which information is accessed at the speed of a keystroke. The programming process also requires the person familiarize themselves with the concept of testing and debugging as well as learning how to maintain the source code. This is also a part of software development. Have you ever wanted to learn how to create your own video game for your personal computer? Well, one would have to learn about computer programming and its many requirements.

Developing software has many phases, one of which is programming. Some consider programming to be an art form while others consider it to be a discipline of engineering. However, there is no reason it cannot be both as well as considered a craft, of sorts. Of course, there is no documentation or any sort of government regulation that is required in order to consider one's self a programmer. This means that it is fairly easy to teach one's self the discipline. Yet, one can only go so far in the job market with a self-proclaimed title of 'programmer'.

The history of programming extends far beyond that of the modern age in which the first computer was actually built. As stated before, programming is an act of problem solving by use of algorithms. There is no requirement that this must be done by use of a computer. Most ancient cultures utilized algebra, geometry, and basic arithmetic in solving problems. However, the first known calculator, aside from the abacus used in ancient Sumeria, was the Antikythera mechanism. It was invented in Greece in the year 100 B.C. It is the first known calculator in existence. The Antikythera mechanism used different sized gears arranged in a specific manner to perform mathematical calculations, but was mostly used to track the lunar and solar movements for calendars.

Later on, Al-Jazari, who was a Kurdish scientist in medieval times, built what was called an automata in 1206. This device was more for entertainment as it operated percussion instruments. Through history, others have tried to create their own machines to top the one before it, but the first official computer program was written by Ada Lovelace. She built a machine that calculated a specific sequence of what is called Bernoulli numbers. Bernoulli numbers are rational numbers placed in a sequence and are connected to the number theory. This creation was what led to modern day computer programming.

In 1945, John von Neumann designed the first electronic digital computer with a processing unit as well as other basic parts that served as a reference for modern day computers. This was the first instance of binary notation and the first of modern day computer code by entering abbreviations rather than symbolic form. This made assembly language faster and less prone to mistakes. Nine years later, the first high level programming language would be invented. It was called FORTRAN. It could specify calculations with the entrance of formulas such as 'y=4x+6x+9'. The program text would often convert this formula into a compiler. A compiler is a set of programs that turns the source code into a source language into the target language. It is often represented in binary code, or a series of zeros and ones, that the computer can understand.

It was not until the 1960's that data storage devices became available. Computer terminals grew less expensive which allowed programs to be added directly to the computers which caused text editors to be created. These allowed corrections to be made without a lot of complicated punched cards. As time passed, more and more programming languages were created. Granted, these more detailed program languages resulted in higher cost of overhead, they allowed computers to operate at much greater speeds which balanced the cost.

In this high-tech world with population booming near seven billion people, programming skills have become almost a daily requirement. Many schools have placed computers in the classrooms or have given each student their own laptop. Some schools even allow those in kindergarten to have iPads©. Children are learning more and more about how to operate programs and even basic concepts of computer programming. Some of these basic requirements are reliability, robustness, usability, portability, maintainability, and performance.

The reliability and robustness of a computer program pertain to how often the results are accurate and how well a program foresees problems due to mistakes. These mistakes are not inclusive of any bugs that the program may contain, but are due to human error in the program. The reliability depends on how correct the algorithms are.

Usability is a simple term. Yet, in regard to computer programming, it refers to how easily a person can use the program for the designated intent. If a program has too many issues, either with graphics or even hardware issues, the usability decreases and often renders the program useless.

How much hardware does the computer program require to run? This question pertains to the portability factor of a program. If it requires entirely too much hardware to allow the program to run, then this increases the difficulty of usage as well. If the operating system struggles to compile or interpret the information, it may not run at all.

Some coding programs are entirely open source and object oriented. These types of programs make it easier to modify the program, fix bugs, repair security issues, and adapt to new environments. This increases the efficiency and performance of the program by decreasing processor time, memory space, decrease network bandwidth required, and even decreases how much the user must interact with the program. The phrase, 'less is more', truly applies to programming. The less certain resources a program requires, the better.

Despite all of the other attributes a good coding program requires, the most important is readability. If the person spends entirely too much time attempting to read or modify the current source code and is unable to spend the proper time on writing the source code, it can make it frustrating. Bugs, inefficiencies, and duplicates of the code are often caused by a source program being unreadable. In order to assist with readability, one should remain consistent in one's programming style. Though there are many factors such as different indentation styles, comments, decomposition, and naming conventions, visual programming language can assist in resolving these.

In relation to programming, one must also look to the complexity of one's algorithms. There is a system in which to classify algorithms. This system is referred to as the 'Big O notation'. The 'Big O notation' identifies the use of resources in terms of the algorithms and the input required. Those who are experienced in programming are well aware of the existence of the more well-established algorithms.

Value modeling, implementation, and debugging are all requirements for software development. There are different methods in which a person can approach the tasks of the aforementioned concepts. These methods are: Use Case analysis, agile software development, Object Oriented Analysis and Design, Model Driven Architecture, and Unified Modeling Language.

The *Use Case Analysis* is often one of the most popular methods for a requirement analysis. It is a list of steps that define the interactions between roles. The purpose is to use those steps to achieve a specific goal. It is often similar to Unified Modeling Language in that the 'role' is known as an 'actor'. However, the 'actor' can be a human, external system, or even time itself. Use Case Analysis has been used in software for the past twenty years. It is also a preferable fit for Agile Software Development.

Agile Software Development is more than a single method, but rather a collaboration of methods in which requirements evolve. It uses a sort of 'cross-functional team' ideology along with self-organization. It is constantly adapting and breaks tasks into smaller and more easily managed increments. Some of these increments do not involve any sort of long-term planning requirements, but still contribute to the end goal. The philosophy behind agile software development is that it is meant to be applicable to larger and more complex projects. These projects often have non-linear characteristics in which accurate estimates are next to impossible during the early stages of the method. As most methods for development of software exist on a spectrum between adaptive programs and predictive programs, the agile development method tends to favor toward the adaptive end of said spectrum. There is a lot of flexibility inside this particular method in the identification of specific parameters. One of the few constants inside this particular method is expected value versus the cost of the method.

The object oriented analysis and design, also known as the OOAD, pertains to programs such as Ruby, Python, and Perl. Granted, the last two source code programs are not one hundred percent object oriented, they are still considered object oriented. The object oriented analysis and design method is often the most popular approach to the application of the object oriented paradigm. It is also the most popular approach to visual modeling and encourages better communication as well as provides a better quality for the final product. Each stage of object oriented analysis and design 'falls' into the next as if it were a waterfall. Each stage has concrete boundaries and requirements that must be met prior to 'falling' into the next stage. Barry Boehm made popular a spiral model that closely resembled the premise for OOAD. The borders between the two are often blurry. Regardless, analysis and design are often performed simultaneously. There is a principle called the 'open/closed principle' that also applies to object oriented analysis and design. The module within the source code is considered open if it is able to support the extension that is created. The opposite is true when it is considered 'closed'. OOAD is divided into three parts: Object oriented analysis, object oriented design, and object oriented modeling.

The object analysis has but one main purpose. That purpose is to create a model of the requirements that the system needs to function without any of the constraints of the implementation. The approach to this type of analysis is that the analysis takes place with specific objects as it integrates the processes and the data in real world situations. Unlike other methods, which consider process and data as separate entities, object analysis treats the two as if they were one in the same. Also, with object analysis, the tasks are to find and organize the objects as well as describe how the object interacts inside the system. An accurate description of the behavior and the internals are often required in the form of a definition.

Object oriented design is the application of the implementation toward the model itself. Often, this includes both software and hardware as well as other requirements such as usability. As previously discussed, the usability of a method could easily render the entire coding program useless or useful. The concepts are mapped and the interfaces result in a model of how the system is to be built. In order to fully grasp the concept and method of object oriented design, one must also familiarize themselves with the software architecture, patterns, and design with the principles.

When one approaches the concept of object oriented modeling, or OOM, one often uses the paradigm through the entire life cycle of the development itself. OOM is often divided in two aspects of work. These aspects are the modeling of behaviors such as use cases and the modeling of static structures such as the different components. Two of the most common components are unified modeling language, which has already been defined as a similar structure to the use case analysis, and the sysML which was described previously as well.

Some of the benefits of the object oriented modeling are that the communication involved is often highly effective. Most people have a hard time understanding the documents and programming codes. Object oriented modeling allows the user to use visual aids.

To give a better idea of why some may have a difficult time understanding the code, it is the same as how some individuals understand algebra better while some have a stronger grasp of geometry. The basic principles are the same, but geometry gives one a stronger advantage through visual aids. With geometry, the person can see what the equation pertains to in real world uses. Object oriented modeling is based loosely on the same concept as geometry. Some people need a tangible concept to hold on to in order to fully comprehend an idea or structure. It fills the 'gap' between the theoretical system and the real world.

Coding is often aided by modeling. Some people must first be able to identify 'what' the problem is before understanding 'how' to solve the problem. This is no different in regard to computer programming. Object oriented modeling assists with creating detailed designs and codes inside of a budget, which is often the primary goal in creating a string of codes for a program. Object oriented modeling produces abstract descriptions as well as accessible descriptions of the system requirements. The models come to define the required structures and often behave in the same manner as processes and objects. Often, it does this above complex source codes.

Source Code

Source code is the foundation of which any program rests upon. It is a collection of specific and specialized instructions appearing in text form. Sometimes, a source code will have comments attached to it in order for the programmer to better understand. It facilitates the work that the computer is supposed to perform. A compiler program often translates source code into binary code in order for the machine to easily understand the commands.

For example, let us take a look at a standard computer application. These contain what are called 'executable files' and those files often have a '.exe' behind it. One such example would be internet explorer. Internet explorer is one of the most common programs used on a computer. Nearly every single person in a developed world has access to the internet. Some may use other programs such as Mozilla Firefox, Google Chrome, or even Silverlight, but Internet Explorer is one of the oldest internet programs. Anyhow, if one was to look up the files inside of the program, one would see something like this: iexplorer.exe. This file is created with a source code that the compiler translates into the binary code the moment you click on the icon for internet explorer and instruct the computer to open the program. However, the source code is not included in the program, but has already been translated by the programmer upon installation. However, there is a process called decompilation that helps a person take an executable program and generate the original source code through assembly or other methods which include a higher level language.

The purpose of a source code, as previously mentioned, is to create the executable program as well as communicate algorithms between individuals.

Oftentimes, programmers will look over and study source codes that already exist prior to creating their own. They look at the techniques in order to contribute to the maturation of their own skills. This is why many programmers share codes among one another.

Software reusability is also a concept many programmers employ. In this concept, people will take one piece of code from a previously established software program and adapt it to function alongside the code for other projects. Yet, the quality of a code will always rest with the purpose of that code. Because of this, most often, readability is less important.

One thing to remember is that hackers are usually self-taught programmers. Unfortunately, the Supreme Court ruled in 2003 that source code is free speech which is protected by the United States Constitution. Many people argued this because it conveys information to programmers and can be used to share information.

Hackers will obtain this information after decompiling the executable function of the information to get ahold of personal information.

However, those *for* the ruling were such people as Dan Bernstein. Bernstein was a math professor at the University of California. He developed and published a source code for an encryption program that he developed. Usually, encryption programs and their algorithms were considered property of the United States government. Bernstein felt it was a free speech issue while the government claimed it was a matter of national security. This would require that, prior to publication, Bernstein would have had to gain approval through the State Department. This led to source coding being protected by the First Amendment due to a lawsuit filed on Bernstein's behalf.

The Beginning

Dozens of programs exist—all with different purposes such as graphic design, server functions, websites, and general computer applications for operating systems and its platforms. Many of these programs are object oriented. This means that memory locations having values likely referenced by an identifier exist. The locations are objects or structures of data. These structures of data refer to the ways that data is organized to operate at the fullest potential. Coding programs such as C++, C#, Python, Java, and many others are object-oriented as well as class based. Another object oriented coding program that is not as well-known is called Ruby.

Ruby is an object-oriented programming language that was created in 1993, but later released in the year 1994 by a man named Yukihiro (Matsumoto) Matsumoto. Matsumoto was born on April 14, 1965 in the Osaka Prefecture, Japan. He taught himself computer programming until he completed high school. From there, he obtained his science degree from the University of Tsukuba. He was also a member of Ikuo Nakata's research lab which was dedicated to computer programming languages.

Matsumoto was later employed by a Japanese open source company. He is also known to have released several open source products such as cmail. It was not long before he created Ruby. Ruby happens to be the only piece of software that was known beyond the borders of Japan.

Matsumoto was familiar with other languages such as Python and Perl, but he felt that those programming languages were not as complete as they could have been nor did they stand up to their reputations for being object oriented. Since Matsumoto felt that there were no other programs in existence that were truly object oriented, he decided to create his own. He called this program 'Ruby'. Even though Matsumoto felt the other programs used were more complex, poorly constructed, or too simplistic and not meeting his needs, wants and expectations as a programmer, Matsumoto, knowing what he was looking for, took what he knew and understood from Python and Perl and their syntax and elements for the inspiration behind Ruby to make a more user friendly and enjoyable experience and to meet his own satisfactions. Ruby is a purely object-oriented language, meaning everything in it is an object, and every object has a class; classes and objects will be explained later.

During an online discussion with his colleague, Yukihiro (Matsumoto) Matsumoto discussed the possibility of an object – oriented program. Matsumoto searched for a program matching his desire, but could not find anything. Failing in his search he decided to make his own, Ruby was born. Matsumoto designed Ruby in in 1993 and released it in 1914. Ruby, which is a purely object-oriented scripting language, was created because he felt other programs he knew and used were more complex, poorly constructed, or too simplistic. Matsumoto took what he knew from how Perl and Python operated, using their syntax for inspiration, and designed Ruby to be more user friendly. He wanted the program to be more enjoyable in its use and ensured that it met his own satisfaction standards. This meant that in order for Ruby to be purely an object oriented language, everything had to be an object.

The name was given to 'Ruby' during an online discussion between Matsumoto and a colleague by the name of Keiju Ishitsuka prior to the code having actually been written. There were two names the pair was considering naming the open source program. Those names were 'Coral' and 'Ruby'. The name 'ruby' was chosen as the namesake of a close colleague's birthstone.

Ruby was first released in Japan to the Japanese media in late 1995. Within two more days, three more versions of Ruby were released. There were other stages of development with the later versions of Ruby. These stages of development included different object oriented designs, classes, mix-ins, and many others.

With the earlier releases, this led to articles being published about Ruby on the internet. Matsumoto was later hired by netlab the same year that the articles were being published which was 1997.

Later in 1999, the first language mailing list in English

began. This showed that there was interest in Ruby beyond the borders of Japan. It was also in 1999 that the first book about Ruby was published titled, *The Object Oriented Scripting Language Ruby*. The following year, twenty more books on the open source programming language would be published in Japanese.

As time passed, Ruby surpassed Python in popularity which spawned the publication of *Programming Ruby*. This was released to the public for no cost which led to a greater and widening adoption of Ruby in the Western world. By 2002, the English mailing lists for Ruby exceeded the number of messages received by the Japanese mailing lists.

In August of 2003, Ruby 1.8 was released. Ruby 1.8 was used by several different industries. The language specifications were developed by a Japanese government agency in order to submit to the Japanese Industrial Standards. Later, it was made to submit to the International Organization for Standardization. This meant it was widely accepted and was subsequently credited for increasing awareness of the product. It was quite stable for a long period of time and was not retired until June of 2013. However, some of the coding within Ruby 1.8 is compatible with the current of Ruby 1.9.

Ruby 1.9 was released before 1.8 was retired. The release of Ruby 1.9 was in 2007. There was a later version, Ruby 1.9.3, that was released in 2011. Despite the advantages of Ruby 1.9, there were many changes to Ruby 1.8 that were being made which caused the delay in popularity for Ruby 1.9.

Despite the delay caused by those changes thus causing the delay in popularity, Ruby 1.9 was undergoing its own changes. Some of these changes included the following:

- block local variables
- additional lambda syntax
- per string character encodings
- new socket API
- import security

Ruby 2.0 was intended to be one hundred percent compatible with Ruby 1.9.3, but this was not the case. Though the majority of Ruby 2.0 was compatible with Ruby 1.9.3, there were noted to be at least five incompatibilities. With Ruby 2.0, there were also added features. These features were: method keyword arguments, new method for extending the class, a new literal for creating an array of symbols, a new API which served the purpose of lazy evaluation of Enumerals, and a new convention of using the hashtag symbol followed by 'to' then underscore and the letter 'h' appearing as such: #to_h.

Ruby 2.1 and 2.2 were later created and released exactly one year apart from each other with Ruby 2.1 being released December 25, 2013 and Ruby 2.2 being released the following year. Ruby 2.1

included bug fixes and library updates as well as utilized semantic versioning. Ruby 2.2, which is also the most recent version, turned out to be the bigger release of the two. It included some of the same updates similar to those of Ruby 2.1, but also included so much more such as deprecated APIs. However, the most noted of introductions of Ruby 2.2 were the changes to how it handled memory, incremental garbage collector, support for that garbage collector, support for the collection of symbols, and the option for the programmer to compile symbols against the jemalloc. It also contains some of the support for using vfork with the system and support for Unicode 7.

The philosophy behind the creation of Ruby is called the 'principle of least astonishment'. This means that it was designed to ease confusion for those who were experienced with coding. It was also meant to be enjoyable for those interested in computer programming by reducing the actual 'work' a programmer often was required to do when setting up codes and functions.

The final version of Ruby has many different features—some which are shared with previous versions, but designed with the best of all previous versions. Ruby is one hundred percent object oriented and allows inheritance, mix ins, and metaclasses (larger classes). It allows two different types of typing called dynamic typing and duck typing. In the current version of Ruby 2.2, everything (including statements) are considered to be expressions.

In addition to that, everything is executed as well as declarations. The syntax is flexible and also serves as a foundation for domain specific languages. Domain specific languages are those languages which are specific to a certain grouping or application domain in contrast to a general purpose language. The use of domain specific languages are in reference to HTML for web pages.

Ruby 2.2 also allows an easy method for altering objects which, in turn, allows the programmer to perform some metaprogramming. There is a unique block of syntax that allows functions such as lexical closures in addition to literal notation for arrays, hashtags, and other symbols. Interpolation, or the embedding of code within a string, are also supported. The four scopes of variables, which will be given in detail later, are supported and denoted by sigils, but sigils are not required.

In addition to the other added benefits of Ruby 2.2, there are many more that can be listed. Ruby 2.2 provides exception handling, operator overloading, a built-in support for handling rational numbers as well as complex numbers. It also allows for a more arbitrarily precise arithmetic. Native threads and cooperative figures are one of its more noted features, as well as the initial support for unicode and other character codings. There is also an interactive Ruby shell, which is also called an REPL. Ruby has also been implemented on all major platforms and has a large standard library. Some of the more familiar modules in that library are 'http', 'openSSL', and 'RSS'. Many laypersons are familiar with those three because they all pertain to the internet. HTTP and HTTPS are always listed before one types in the 'www' preceding the web address.

HTTP stands for hypertext transfer protocol. It is an application protocol for information systems and is the foundation of data communication for the World Wide Web, which is the 'www' in every web address. It is a structured text that uses the hyperlinks between the nodes of text. The only difference between HTTP and HTTPS is that the latter is considered to be more secure than the former.

Ruby allows procedural programming that defines functions and variables outside of the classes which makes those functions and variables part of the object itself.

There is no one-way to install ruby. Ruby is open source and there are a lot of third party tools to use. You can use package managers, installers, and you can also build Ruby from source. It is recommended, however, that should a person desire to learn more about the installation process of Ruby, the official website is the best place to gain that valuable information.

Programming languages all consist of virtually the same elements: classes, strings, arrays, variables, etc. The difference with

Ruby is, as mentioned earlier, is it is purely an object oriented programming language and every value is an object.

Ruby comes with what is called an 'I.R.B' or interactive Ruby, which is installed when an individual installs Ruby. I.R.B is an interactive environment that enables real time interaction so the individual can test theoretical codes. This is a great tool because it allows the programmer to experiment with his or her code in real time and see what it will do without affecting the work in progress. In order to access I.R.B on a Mac, go to your utilities folder and open the terminal application. By initiating I.R.B, simply type it into the command line and your experimental coding beings. For windows this will be the command prompt located in your accessories folder, or by holding the windows key and pressing "R" for the run box to appear, then type cmd which is programming shorthand for 'command'.

For an example, let us say you are working on code. You have an idea or two as to what may help fix the problem, but you hesitate because you do not want to put those codes into your current project. So, I.R.B opens an interactive environment so the individual can test those theories without disturbing the code scripts in the active project which allows the individual to solve the problem.

However, if the individual is new to using Ruby or even programming in general, the person can use an easier version of the

I.R.B by typing irb-simple-prompt. This is the same thing, but the prompt does not number your lines thus making it easier for the user to visualize.

Syntax

Just like every language, Ruby has a particular way that it fuses together and operates. Because Matsumoto based Ruby's syntax on the syntax from Perl and Python, the program is very particular just as the previously aforementioned. However, one difference between Perl and Ruby is that Perl requires that variables be prefixed with a sigil. A sigil is a symbol that is attached to the name of a variable which shows the variables scope. For example, if a variable is shown as '$abc', the sigil is the dollar sign. Python and Perl also does not keep all of its instance variables completely private, but Ruby does. C++ and Java cannot be created with a single line of code, but Ruby has the ability to do so through a process known as metaprogramming. Metaprogramming is defined as an ability to treat programs as their data. Basically, a program could be designed for a specific purpose, such as to read other programs, and metaprogramming would allow this program to modify itself while running.

Similarities between Python and Ruby are that Python's descriptors are very similar. However, the tradeoff happens in the development process. If one should desire to use Python to create a code and desires later to change that code from public to private, the code internal to the class will need to be adjusted. This is not so in Ruby as Ruby's design makes all instance variables private while providing an easy way to declare set and methods.

Despite the fact that it may sound difficult to a person unfamiliar with programming, Ruby was developed to be a fun and enjoyable experience as well as fairly simple. The individual should also keep in mind objects in Ruby are case sensitive, 'RUBY' and 'ruby' will mean two completely different things to the program's compiler. The syntax in Ruby consists of whitespaces, which are spaces between the objects (words, letters, numbers, and symbols) tabs. These objects are typically ignored unless those objects are placed within a string. Semicolons and newline characters indicate the end of a statement unless those items are followed by an operator of sort. This indicates to the program that the statement, or function, will continue. Comments are items that are typed in when the programmer needs to leave notes for themselves or another individual. When writing a comment in Ruby, the person uses the hashtag symbol followed by the comment. For example, one would enter the following: `#this is a comment.`

Ruby's compiler will ignore reading this as part of the code and will only be seen as a comment in the code.

Differences

Some of the main differences between programs such as C or Perl and Ruby are quite notable. For example, the language syntax is, as previously mentioned, case sensitive. This means that if you use the capital letter 'A' somewhere in the code for a specific purpose, you must always use the capital version of said letter—just as with the word BEGIN and begin. Both, in spoken language, mean the same thing. In an internet chat room, the former would be as if someone was shouting. However, in programming, they are two separate meanings.

Also, in Ruby, sigils of the dollar sign and the 'at' sign indicate scope resolution operators rather than variable data type which occurs in Perl. Floating point literals are required to have numerical digits on both sides of the decimal point. For example, one cannot denote '.5' by that alone, but must denote it as such, '0.5'. Integer literals can have methods that apply to them. Requiring a digit to precede the decimal point or come after a decimal point makes it easier to understand whether they should be parsed or used as an exponential in the floating format.

Boolean data types are allowed in Boolean contexts in Ruby as opposed to programs such as Smalltalk and Java. However, the mapping are different. The number zero and the word 'empty' in such instances as an empty list or associative array evaluate themselves as true which in turn changes the meaning of some of the common idioms in programs such as Perl or Lisp.

In Ruby, all constants are considered to be objects or refer to objects. These change what a constant refers to and usually creates some sort of warning. However, making alterations to the object itself does not create a warning. This happens with Ruby 1.9 and is similar to the final variables in Java. The main difference in this is that Ruby can provide the ability to 'freeze' and object. Java cannot perform that function.

Interactive Ruby Shell

The interactive Ruby shell is one of the most impressive attributes to Ruby. It is also the basis for what makes Ruby work as it does. It is the essence of the object oriented scripting language. The reason that the abbreviation for Interactive Ruby Shell is 'I.R.B' is that the filename extension for Ruby is '.rb'. Ruby is launged from a simple command line. The execution of Ruby allows commands with an instantaneous response and therefore allows the individual to experiment with the code in what is called 'real time'. The features of the Interactive Ruby Shell are as such that it allows the tracking of a command history, the ability to edit lines, job control, and the ability to communicate as a shell script over the internet with a live server.

Implementations

Matsumoto created a program bears the responsibility of implementation and interpreting the actions of Ruby. It is often referred to as MRI which stands for Matz's Ruby Interpreter. It is written using C, but uses its own virtual machine to perform its function. This was used in Ruby 1.8. However, Ruby 1.9, Ruby 1.9.3, 2.0, and the most recent version of Ruby 2.1 use what is called YARV. YARV stands for 'yet another Ruby VM'. This has far surpassed the slower virtual machine, or VM.

Since the year 2010, Ruby has been released with several different implementations. A few of these implementations are as follows: Jruby, IronRuby, MacRuby, and RubyMotion just to name a few. Jruby is a Java version that runs on the Java VM. MacRuby and RubyMotion are similar implementations with one major difference. MacRuby runs on Macs, but the iOS version is RubyMotion. This means that it runs with other Apple© products that use the Apple operating system.

IronRuby operates on a .NET framework. The .NET framework was developed by Microsoft with its initial release in 2002. It runs best with Microsoft Windows and is adaptable to many different programming languages such as IronRuby. There are several programs that were written for the .NET framework that operates across several different programming languages. This is called a CLR, or Common Language Runtime. It is an application that handles the security, memory, and exceptions within an application The FCL, or Framework Class Network, and the CLR make up the .NET framework.

IronRuby and the .NET

To further explore some of these implementations, IronRuby specifically targets the .NET framework. It runs in tandem with the DLR, or Dynamic Language Runtime which is a library that runs in tandem with the Common Language Infrastructure. What this does is provide dynamic typing as well as method dispatch for dynamic languages.

In 2007, the DLR design team presented a version of the IronRuby compiler at OSCON. OSCON is short for 'operating systems convention'. The team struggled to get IronRuby to support Rails. Despite the fact that the functional tests did run, there was still a lot of work left to do in order to be able to get the program to work in a production environment.

IronRuby runs well on both Mono and Microsoft's CLR. However, these results only proved successful in the testing environment. Since the inoperability between the two proved to be limited, there is better support for other dynamic languages.

Silverlight was later created and supports IronRuby, but is used as a scripting engine similar to that of JamaScript. They are passed via script tags as noted in the example below:

```
//DLR initiation script.
<script src=http://
gestalt.ironruby.net/dlr-latest.js"
type="text/javascript>


//Client-side script passed to
IronRuby and Silverlight.
<script type="text/ruby">
        window.Alert("Hello from Ruby")
</script>
```
(Example Citation: en.m.wikipedia.org/wiki/IronRuby)

Currently, there is an integration between IronRuby and RubySpec. RubySpec is a project that allows Ruby to write complete specifications for the Ruby Programming Language.

Directories:

A directory is simply a file path in a computer in which whatever file you are working on or save is stored. Ruby also has directories built within it that houses it's tools and elements.

Blocks:

When an individual is working in any programming language, you create what is called a block or blocks of code. A block of code is basically the entire embodiment of your code between braces or do-end. It consists of statements, variables, strings, arrays, expressions, methods, and everything else that makes up the code that tells your computer what to do. Ruby does not execute the code at the same time it is encountered, but instead remembers the context in which the block appears. For example:

Prints "hello everyone\n"

This is an example of a very basic block of code, not very much, but it contains your object/variable and the method used to produce the results "hello everyone". Once the code it processed, the quotations will not be included as part of the results.

Classes:

A class serves as a blue print for objects. Ruby and other programming languages like it have classes already built in. However as you work on your code, you can create your own classes as well. As you type your code, you are creating either a single object or a list of objects. As these objects are created, you may need them for other parts of your program which is when you will need to call for a class, in this case, a class you created. You can define a class and call for the class later in your code when needed. When you create a class, always use a capital letter for the class name.

An example of this is the following:

```
class Cat
    def initialize(breed, name)
        # Instance variables
        @breed = breed
        @name = name
    end

    def mew
        puts 'Meow! Meow!'
    end

    def display

```

```
    puts "I am of #{@breed} breed and my name
is #{@name}"
☐    end
☐  end
```

Variables:

As mentioned above, a variable is an object with an assigned value. Variables are called variables simply because their values can change, their values can be whatever is required of the program. For instance in Algebra, we assign value to x plus y equals seven. The value of x and the value of y are defined by variables of different numbers that all equal to seven. Pairs of numbers that equal to seven can be substituted for the letters x and y. Variables can also be used to assign a description of an object rather than a number. If you are working on a program, or a game for instance that involves cars and driving. In order to add color value to the vehicle in the game, the person would do the following:

Driver\'s_car = red.

So now when you run your program, the farmer's barn will be colored red. The underscore (_) is used to make it easier to map your object throughout your code; we will discuss mapping later. But that is the basics of a variable: a variable is a placeholder for a value; think of it as a briefcase holding an item.

Ruby provides four types of variables. The first of these variables are called local variables. Local variables are defined in a method. If you recall, a method (in regard to computer programming) is the procedure that is associated with the object class. Local variables often begin with a lowercase letter or an underscore.

The second variable that Ruby provides is called an 'instance variable'. These variables are available across all methods for instances or objects—meaning that these variables change from object to object. They are usually preceded by the 'at' sign and followed by the name of the variable.

The third variable is called a class variable. It is available across the different objects as well, but belongs to the class as it has characteristics of that class. They are usually preceded in coding by *two* of the 'at' symbols and followed by the name of the variable.

The fourth and final variable is called the global variable. These class-style variables are not available across the different classes. If an individual wants to have a single variable, the global variable must be defined. If you recall, single variables are available across the classes. The way to identify the global variable in a string of coding is that the global variable is preceded by the dollar symbol.

Reserved Words

In regard to coding in general and creating the strings of syntax, a specific set of words has been created that is widely accepted among all types of open source coding. These words are called reserved words. They are not meant to be used to create classes, however, nor are they meant to be used as constants and variables. They simply direct the action of the syntax. Some examples are shown below:

- BEGIN: This code is enclosed in brackets and usually is the identification of the beginning of the code.
- END: This code is in all caps, enclosed in brackets, and tells the program when to end.

- Alias: An alias is created specifically for operators, global variables or a method already in existence
- and: this word is used in a string of syntax and represented by the symbol &&. It is also a logical operator, but takes a lower precedence.
- Break: In lowercase form, the word will terminate a command until the next entry is made within a string of syntax.
- /case: The backslash followed by the word 'case' in lowercase letters compares an expression with a matching within a clause.

- <u>Class:</u>   This word, in all lowercase letters, defines a class within a string of syntactical code and can only cease with the word 'end'.

Objects

With most programming languages, objects are created. However, Ruby was designed to be completely object oriented. This means that the items that one would use are already considered objects. If one recalls, objects have a variable and objects. Since Ruby is one hundred percent object oriented, it already contains the necessary variables which have the values required to function. In Ruby, all things are objects and have a value, but not all are variables. Since this only covers the elements already associated with Ruby, a person will still need to create their own objects and assign values to those objects. When the person begins typing the desired code, the items are the subjects of the program the programmer wishes to be recognized. For instance, if a person is doing a mathematical program such as 'a+b', the programmer determines what both 'a' and 'b' stand for—or better what, what the values of 'a' and 'b' are. In the program screen, the programmer will do this as such:

a=2

b=5

This is called assigning value to the operator by using the equal (=) operator. Now, both objects have been assigned a value. When the program is ran with the desired mathematical notations through one of four identified functions (addition, subtraction, multiplication, or division), the person will get the desired results associated with said desired notation.

Once the values of the objects are defined, the programmer can create classes in which to store said values. If one would refer to the aforementioned 'cat' example, of which the programmer can add another part of the program by 'calling' it when needed, the person could create a class by using one of the many 'reserved words' discussed earlier.

Statements

In regard to programming, a statement is the smallest part of a program in which the programmer can write and still make the compiler produce desired results. Though a person can still write a simple program such as 'Hello everyone' and the compiler will still produce the aforementioned results, a statement can consist of identifiers, expressions, arrays, strings, and many other elements. In many other languages, statements are ended with a semicolon to signal to the compiler the end of the desired statements. However, semicolons are not required by Ruby. Ruby utilizes different ending to statements, but a person still can use a semicolon if desired. An example would be as follows:

```
$ I.R.B
>> puts "Hello, Dolly!"
Hello Dolly
=>nil
```

As you can see, the statement is short and sweet, but does not end with a semicolon. Rather, it begins with the dollar sign, which we learned earlier is associated with the I.R.B. It also ends with the equal sign, the top of an arrow, and the word 'nil'.

Strings

As with everything else in Ruby, a string is an object. More importantly, a string is a holder of char data, or character data. This means that the string is designed to store arbitrary collections, or sequences of digits, letters, whitespaces, or symbols, that are assembled together. Unlike arrays, a string is not fixed. It can change if it is a character pointer (a way to 'call' or point to another string). The length of a string is the number of characters. It contains the plus symbol, one, and a null character. A null character is simply a character that returns to zero value which terminates the string thus ending that process. The simplest of string literals are found to be enclosed by a single set of quotations. The text within those quotations becomes the falue of that string—very similar to the value of a variable. If an apostrophe is needed, the backslash symbol is used just before the apostrophe. This will prevent the compiler from believing the statement has been terminated. Another thing that makes the string literals different from an array is that the strong literals appear in the form of a list rather than side by side. An example of this is:

'hello everyone'

'how are you'

'I am good thanks'

Remember, Ruby is sensitive about the way code is typed in, so be cautious and aware of punctuations and capitalization that you put into your program as you are typing your code.

Arrays:

An array is a list of objects you create when you are typing your code. They are read in order and separated simply by adding a comma between them, much like how "prints" will display results as we viewed earlier. It is the exact same as with writing from a grammatical point of view in which a person separates a list of objects by a comma. Each of the above is a variable with a stored value in them, and they are listed side by side separated by a comma. As mentioned in the section about strings, arrays are fixed objects and cannot be changed.

Any time you are writing a code and you want something to display on the screen as a result, you type either print or puts (put string). The difference between print and puts is that typing in 'puts' will display your results in a list format very similar to strings whereas putting in the word 'print' will not do so. Let us say that you wish to tell Ruby to display a work on the screen twice. The word 'print' will instruct the Ruby compiler to display the word two times. 'Put' will display the results in a list format.

Comments:

Often when writing a code, you may want to leave a comment or a note for yourself or another who may look at the code to let them know something. Comments are made by using the hashtag symbol. As previously mentioned, comments are not ready by the compiler as part of the string of code, but are stored in the classes for the moment that someone wishes to access them.

Identifiers:

An identifier is used to identify variables, methods, and classes. Identifiers are made of up alphanumerical characters and underscores (_), but do not begin with a digit. Identifiers that are used to name methods may end with a question mark (?), exclamation point (!), or equals sign (=). Reserved words may also be used as identifiers. There are not restrictions for the length or size of your identifiers, only what your computers memory is able to handle.

Methods:

A method is a block of code that is associated with one or more objects. When you have written a block of code, you can define it as a method using a defining operator. This way, when one is writing a code and desires to instruct one part of said code to perform one particular action and the other perform something different, the programmer an invoke or call the name, or identify the other block of code within the first code.

An example of defining a method is as follows:
*def method_name(arg_list, *list_expr, &block_expr)*
expr..
end
 # singleton method
*def expr.identifier(arg_list, *list_expr, &block_expr)*
expr..
end

The phrase 'def' is called the defining operation which defines the variable and the word 'end' ends the statement, if one were to refer to the list of reserved words.

Expressions:

In coding, an expression is the result of an operation. For example, when a person adds value to a variable, it can be considered a literal, a variable reference, and a method invocation. It is very similar to writing a mathematical equation. In essence, they are the same. For example, let us use the mathematical expression of $x+y=5$. The equal sign is the operator which instructs the values of 'x' and 'y' to be equal to the number five. The number five, which is a result of the two variables, is the expression. So, anytime a person has variables or some form of objects that end with a result, the result itself is the expression.

Operators:

When an individual is writing a code, it is obvious that there is a purpose behind it. However, the code cannot function alone. If required the command to do as the programmer wishes, the programmer must embed operators. Operators are parts within the code that instruct the code to perform specific functions. For example, if the person wanted the variables x, y, and z which represent the values of one, two, and three to add up to a specific sum, the programmer would need to use the addition operator (or the plus sign). See the example below:

x+y+z

The letter x, y, and z, as previously stated, represent the variables. Now, let us give the letters x, y, and z a value by substituting the numbers one, two, and three:

1+2+3

Now, the programmer has given the values an operator telling them to create a sum which adds up to the sum of six.

Regular expression modifiers often include items called 'optional modifiers' that control the different aspects of matching and comes after the second backslash character. It can be represented by the following characters: I, o, x, m, u, e, s, and n. The letter 'I' instructs the code to ignore the case of the letters when matching the text. The letter 'o' performs the hashtag and bracket interpolations once. The letter 'x' allows the code to ignore the presence of whitespace. It also allows the programmer to put comments inside of the regular expression. The letter 'm' matches many lines and recognizes new lines as normal characters. The letters 'u', 'e', 's', and 'n' all interpret the regular expression as unicode as well as others. However, if none of the modifiers happen to be specified, those variables use the source coding.

Similar to string literals that have been delimited, Ruby allows the programmer to begin with regular expressions with the percent sign followed by the lowercase letter 'r' (%r) to be followed by a delimiter of one's choice. The ability to do this is useful when the pattern the programmer is describing contains many forward slash characters that the programmer does not wish to escape.

More About Ruby and Computer Languages

Ruby is very similar to Visual BASIC due to the markup script that both use, yet Ruby is not used as often as C++ and others. Wikipedia, via WikiUniversity, offers a course on Ruby and other programming languages. In order to take the course, WikiUniversity recommends that the individual have Ruby installed on their computer, read books that introduce the reader to programming and programming logic, and read books about object oriented programming.

Conclusion

Computer programming has come a long way throughout history. From ancient Sumeria and Ancient Greece to the first calculator as well as to the first punch-card coding system, Ruby came to be developed with the user in mind. It is the first of its kind, developed in Japan, but it was also the first of its kind to take the world on by storm. Many programming enthusiasts as well as professional computer programmers have hailed Ruby as one of the easiest to use due to it being an object oriented program. Even the package installer, RubyGem, is easy to use. As many people struggle with Algebraic concepts, but more easily understand those same concepts in Geometry, the Ruby user understands this object oriented program more easily than the alternative. The design pattern is more easily suited for those who program with data. It also reduces the amount of code written and the number of errors and debugging.

Some understand the concepts of Ruby when best described using metaphors. That is most likely because people understand new concepts when related to well-known and established concepts. To sum up the concept of 'class' in regard to Ruby, think of an actor. The first class will be defined in regard to an actor and the attributes of an actor. Actors can be considered to be objects when used in relation to Ruby.

Everything in Ruby has a special key word that is used to create the object. Once the object is created, it can float, string, or have an array. Though programming is designed to reduce repetition, it is acceptable to copy and paste when the classes contain the same attributes. Thus creates a new concept called inheritance. The two classes are then merged in code form.

Instance methods allow one to, code wise, filter out the items that remain undesired. For example, if one has a set of individuals both living and dead but wishes to only acknowledge the ones that are alive, an instance method allows the programmer to use the code that is called an 'instance method'.

To review the abstraction principle in regard to coding and Ruby, specifically, one would enter the data as such:

- require 'time'

class: relative

☐ def age

☐ if alive?

☐ A = Time. Now – time.parse

else

a = time.parse(death_date)

end

Then, the individual programmer would enter the parameters

regarding the subject or group he or she wishes to input the data of.

As time has progressed, Microsoft developed an operating system which would make coding skills nearly obsolete for the regular person. As Windows was developed, all one needed to do to perform a function was to click on an icon. The developers, programmers, and coders who worked for Microsoft developed executable files for each icon represented on the desktop of Windows. Once Windows became a mainstream staple, people began to have less and less knowledge about coding. Yet, now that the new popular thing to do is to create applications for cell phones, coding and programming platforms such as Ruby are coming back in popularity.

Though a lot of programs are object oriented, which means there are memory locations that have values likely referenced by an identifier, these locations are objects, which are ways data is organized to the fullest potential. In addition to that, object oriented and open source coding programs appear to be the most popular formats among the new age programmers. Regardless of current trends, a choice of format or platform is always up to the individual. It is a personal choice and the person should choose the format and platform based on which works best with the individual and will provide the best results.